This Collection of Snark Belongs to:

_____

_____

_____

_____

Date: _____

Today's Garbage Humans:

Today's Garbage Activities:

Lessons Learned From All This Garbage:

At Least The World Still Has:

...For Now.

Today's Ratings: ☆ ☆ ☆ ☆ ☆

Date: _____

Today's Garbage Humans:

Today's Garbage Activities:

Lessons Learned From All This Garbage:

At Least The World Still Has:

...For Now.

Today's Ratings: ☆ ☆ ☆ ☆ ☆

Date: _____

Today's Garbage Humans:

Today's Garbage Activities:

Lessons Learned From All This Garbage:

At Least The World Still Has:

...For Now.

Today's Ratings: ☆ ☆ ☆ ☆ ☆

Date: _____

Today's Garbage Humans:

Today's Garbage Activities:

Lessons Learned From All This Garbage:

At Least The World Still Has:

...For Now.

Today's Ratings: ☆ ☆ ☆ ☆ ☆

Date: _____

Today's Garbage Humans:

Today's Garbage Activities:

Lessons Learned From All This Garbage:

At Least The World Still Has:

...For Now.

Today's Ratings: ☆ ☆ ☆ ☆ ☆
🗑 🗑 🗑 🗑 🗑

Date: _____

Today's Garbage Humans:

Today's Garbage Activities:

Lessons Learned From All This Garbage:

At Least The World Still Has:

...For Now.

Today's Ratings: ☆ ☆ ☆ ☆ ☆
🗑 🗑 🗑 🗑 🗑

Date: _____

Today's Garbage Humans:

Today's Garbage Activities:

Lessons Learned From All This Garbage:

At Least The World Still Has:

...For Now.

Today's Ratings: ☆ ☆ ☆ ☆ ☆

Date: _____

Today's Garbage Humans:

Today's Garbage Activities:

Lessons Learned From All This Garbage:

At Least The World Still Has:

...For Now.

Today's Ratings: ☆ ☆ ☆ ☆ ☆

Date: _____

Today's Garbage Humans:

Today's Garbage Activities:

Lessons Learned From All This Garbage:

At Least The World Still Has:

...For Now.

Today's Ratings: ☆ ☆ ☆ ☆ ☆

Date: _____

Today's Garbage Humans:

Today's Garbage Activities:

Lessons Learned From All This Garbage:

At Least The World Still Has:

...For Now.

Today's Ratings:

Date: _____

Today's Garbage Humans:

Today's Garbage Activities:

Lessons Learned From All This Garbage:

At Least The World Still Has:

...For Now.

Today's Ratings: ☆ ☆ ☆ ☆ ☆
🗑 🗑 🗑 🗑 🗑

Date: _____

Today's Garbage Humans:

Today's Garbage Activities:

Lessons Learned From All This Garbage:

At Least The World Still Has:

...For Now.

Today's Ratings: ☆ ☆ ☆ ☆ ☆
🗑 🗑 🗑 🗑 🗑

Date: _____

Today's Garbage Humans:

Today's Garbage Activities:

Lessons Learned From All This Garbage:

At Least The World Still Has:

...For Now.

Today's Ratings: ☆ ☆ ☆ ☆ ☆
🗑 🗑 🗑 🗑 🗑

Date: _____

Today's Garbage Humans:

Today's Garbage Activities:

Lessons Learned From All This Garbage:

At Least The World Still Has:

...For Now.

Today's Ratings: ☆ ☆ ☆ ☆ ☆

Date: _____

Today's Garbage Humans:

Today's Garbage Activities:

Lessons Learned From All This Garbage:

At Least The World Still Has:

...For Now.

Today's Ratings: ☆ ☆ ☆ ☆ ☆

Date: _____

Today's Garbage Humans:

Today's Garbage Activities:

Lessons Learned From All This Garbage:

At Least The World Still Has:

...For Now.

Today's Ratings:

Date: _____

Today's Garbage Humans:

Today's Garbage Activities:

Lessons Learned From All This Garbage:

At Least The World Still Has:

...For Now.

Today's Ratings: ☆ ☆ ☆ ☆ ☆

Date: _____

Today's Garbage Humans:

Today's Garbage Activities:

Lessons Learned From All This Garbage:

At Least The World Still Has:

...For Now.

Today's Ratings:

Date: _____

Today's Garbage Humans:

Today's Garbage Activities:

Lessons Learned From All This Garbage:

At Least The World Still Has:

...For Now.

Today's Ratings: ☆ ☆ ☆ ☆ ☆
🗑 🗑 🗑 🗑 🗑

Date: _____

Today's Garbage Humans:

Today's Garbage Activities:

Lessons Learned From All This Garbage:

At Least The World Still Has:

...For Now.

Today's Ratings: ☆ ☆ ☆ ☆ ☆
🗑 🗑 🗑 🗑 🗑

Date: _____

Today's Garbage Humans:

Today's Garbage Activities:

Lessons Learned From All This Garbage:

At Least The World Still Has:

...For Now.

Today's Ratings: ☆ ☆ ☆ ☆ ☆
🗑 🗑 🗑 🗑 🗑

Date: _____

Today's Garbage Humans:

Today's Garbage Activities:

Lessons Learned From All This Garbage:

At Least The World Still Has:

...For Now.

Today's Ratings: ☆ ☆ ☆ ☆ ☆

Date: _____

Today's Garbage Humans:

Today's Garbage Activities:

Lessons Learned From All This Garbage:

At Least The World Still Has:

...For Now.

Today's Ratings: ☆ ☆ ☆ ☆ ☆

Date: _____

Today's Garbage Humans:

Today's Garbage Activities:

Lessons Learned From All This Garbage:

At Least The World Still Has:

...For Now.

Today's Ratings: ☆ ☆ ☆ ☆ ☆

Date: _____

Today's Garbage Humans:

Today's Garbage Activities:

Lessons Learned From All This Garbage:

At Least The World Still Has:

...For Now.

Today's Ratings: ☆ ☆ ☆ ☆ ☆
🗑 🗑 🗑 🗑 🗑

Date: _____

Today's Garbage Humans:

Today's Garbage Activities:

Lessons Learned From All This Garbage:

At Least The World Still Has:

...For Now.

Today's Ratings: ☆ ☆ ☆ ☆ ☆

Date: _____

Today's Garbage Humans:

Today's Garbage Activities:

Lessons Learned From All This Garbage:

At Least The World Still Has:

...For Now.

Today's Ratings: ☆ ☆ ☆ ☆ ☆

🗑 🗑 🗑 🗑 🗑

Date: _____

Today's Garbage Humans:

Today's Garbage Activities:

Lessons Learned From All This Garbage:

At Least The World Still Has:

...For Now.

Today's Ratings:

Date: _____

Today's Garbage Humans:

Today's Garbage Activities:

Lessons Learned From All This Garbage:

At Least The World Still Has:

...For Now.

Today's Ratings: ☆ ☆ ☆ ☆ ☆
🗑 🗑 🗑 🗑 🗑

Date: _____

Today's Garbage Humans:

Today's Garbage Activities:

Lessons Learned From All This Garbage:

At Least The World Still Has:

...For Now.

Today's Ratings: ☆ ☆ ☆ ☆ ☆

Date: _____

Today's Garbage Humans:

Today's Garbage Activities:

Lessons Learned From All This Garbage:

At Least The World Still Has:

...For Now.

Today's Ratings: ☆ ☆ ☆ ☆ ☆
🗑 🗑 🗑 🗑 🗑

Date: _____

Today's Garbage Humans:

Today's Garbage Activities:

Lessons Learned From All This Garbage:

At Least The World Still Has:

...For Now.

Today's Ratings:

Date: _____

Today's Garbage Humans:

Today's Garbage Activities:

Lessons Learned From All This Garbage:

At Least The World Still Has:

...For Now.

Today's Ratings: ☆ ☆ ☆ ☆ ☆

Date: _____

Today's Garbage Humans:

Today's Garbage Activities:

Lessons Learned From All This Garbage:

At Least The World Still Has:

...For Now.

Today's Ratings: ☆ ☆ ☆ ☆ ☆

Date: _____

Today's Garbage Humans:

Today's Garbage Activities:

Lessons Learned From All This Garbage:

At Least The World Still Has:

...For Now.

Today's Ratings: ☆ ☆ ☆ ☆ ☆

Date: _____

Today's Garbage Humans:

Today's Garbage Activities:

Lessons Learned From All This Garbage:

At Least The World Still Has:

...For Now.

Today's Ratings: ☆ ☆ ☆ ☆ ☆
🗑 🗑 🗑 🗑 🗑

Date: _____

Today's Garbage Humans:

Today's Garbage Activities:

Lessons Learned From All This Garbage:

At Least The World Still Has:

...For Now.

Today's Ratings: ☆ ☆ ☆ ☆ ☆

🗑 🗑 🗑 🗑 🗑

Date: _____

Today's Garbage Humans:

Today's Garbage Activities:

Lessons Learned From All This Garbage:

At Least The World Still Has:

...For Now.

Today's Ratings:

Date: _____

Today's Garbage Humans:

Today's Garbage Activities:

Lessons Learned From All This Garbage:

At Least The World Still Has:

...For Now.

Today's Ratings: ☆ ☆ ☆ ☆ ☆

Date: _____

Today's Garbage Humans:

Today's Garbage Activities:

Lessons Learned From All This Garbage:

At Least The World Still Has:

...For Now.

Today's Ratings: ☆ ☆ ☆ ☆ ☆

Date: _____

Today's Garbage Humans:

Today's Garbage Activities:

Lessons Learned From All This Garbage:

At Least The World Still Has:

...For Now.

Today's Ratings: ☆ ☆ ☆ ☆ ☆

Date: _____

Today's Garbage Humans:

Today's Garbage Activities:

Lessons Learned From All This Garbage:

At Least The World Still Has:

...For Now.

Today's Ratings: ☆ ☆ ☆ ☆ ☆

Date: _____

Today's Garbage Humans:

Today's Garbage Activities:

Lessons Learned From All This Garbage:

At Least The World Still Has:

...For Now.

Today's Ratings: ☆ ☆ ☆ ☆ ☆

Date: _____

Today's Garbage Humans:

Today's Garbage Activities:

Lessons Learned From All This Garbage:

At Least The World Still Has:

...For Now.

Today's Ratings: ☆ ☆ ☆ ☆ ☆
🗑 🗑 🗑 🗑 🗑

Date: _____

Today's Garbage Humans:

Today's Garbage Activities:

Lessons Learned From All This Garbage:

At Least The World Still Has:

...For Now.

Today's Ratings: ☆ ☆ ☆ ☆ ☆

Date: _____

Today's Garbage Humans:

Today's Garbage Activities:

Lessons Learned From All This Garbage:

At Least The World Still Has:

...For Now.

Today's Ratings: ☆ ☆ ☆ ☆ ☆

Date: _____

Today's Garbage Humans:

Today's Garbage Activities:

Lessons Learned From All This Garbage:

At Least The World Still Has:

...For Now.

Today's Ratings: ☆ ☆ ☆ ☆ ☆
🗑 🗑 🗑 🗑 🗑

Date: _____

Today's Garbage Humans:

Today's Garbage Activities:

Lessons Learned From All This Garbage:

At Least The World Still Has:

...For Now.

Today's Ratings: ☆ ☆ ☆ ☆ ☆

Date: _____

Today's Garbage Humans:

Today's Garbage Activities:

Lessons Learned From All This Garbage:

At Least The World Still Has:

...For Now.

Today's Ratings: ☆ ☆ ☆ ☆ ☆

Date: _____

Today's Garbage Humans:

Today's Garbage Activities:

Lessons Learned From All This Garbage:

At Least The World Still Has:

...For Now.

Today's Ratings: ☆ ☆ ☆ ☆ ☆

Date: _____

Today's Garbage Humans:

Today's Garbage Activities:

Lessons Learned From All This Garbage:

At Least The World Still Has:

...For Now.

Today's Ratings: ☆ ☆ ☆ ☆ ☆

Date: _____

Today's Garbage Humans:

Today's Garbage Activities:

Lessons Learned From All This Garbage:

At Least The World Still Has:

...For Now.

Today's Ratings: ☆ ☆ ☆ ☆ ☆
🗑 🗑 🗑 🗑 🗑

Date: _____

Today's Garbage Humans:

Today's Garbage Activities:

Lessons Learned From All This Garbage:

At Least The World Still Has:

...For Now.

Today's Ratings: ☆ ☆ ☆ ☆ ☆

🗑 🗑 🗑 🗑 🗑

Date: _____

Today's Garbage Humans:

Today's Garbage Activities:

Lessons Learned From All This Garbage:

At Least The World Still Has:

...For Now.

Today's Ratings: ☆ ☆ ☆ ☆ ☆

Date: _____

Today's Garbage Humans:

Today's Garbage Activities:

Lessons Learned From All This Garbage:

At Least The World Still Has:

...For Now.

Today's Ratings: ☆ ☆ ☆ ☆ ☆
🗑 🗑 🗑 🗑 🗑

Date: _____

Today's Garbage Humans:

Today's Garbage Activities:

Lessons Learned From All This Garbage:

At Least The World Still Has:

...For Now.

Today's Ratings: ☆ ☆ ☆ ☆ ☆
🗑 🗑 🗑 🗑 🗑

Date: _____

Today's Garbage Humans:

Today's Garbage Activities:

Lessons Learned From All This Garbage:

At Least The World Still Has:

...For Now.

Today's Ratings: ☆ ☆ ☆ ☆ ☆

Date: _____

Today's Garbage Humans:

Today's Garbage Activities:

Lessons Learned From All This Garbage:

At Least The World Still Has:

...For Now.

Today's Ratings: ☆ ☆ ☆ ☆ ☆

Date: _____

Today's Garbage Humans:

Today's Garbage Activities:

Lessons Learned From All This Garbage:

At Least The World Still Has:

...For Now.

Today's Ratings: ☆ ☆ ☆ ☆ ☆
🗑 🗑 🗑 🗑 🗑

Date: _____

Today's Garbage Humans:

Today's Garbage Activities:

Lessons Learned From All This Garbage:

At Least The World Still Has:

...For Now.

Today's Ratings: ☆ ☆ ☆ ☆ ☆

Date: _____

Today's Garbage Humans:

Today's Garbage Activities:

Lessons Learned From All This Garbage:

At Least The World Still Has:

...For Now.

Today's Ratings: ☆ ☆ ☆ ☆ ☆

Date: _____

Today's Garbage Humans:

Today's Garbage Activities:

Lessons Learned From All This Garbage:

At Least The World Still Has:

...For Now.

Today's Ratings: ☆ ☆ ☆ ☆ ☆

Date: _____

Today's Garbage Humans:

Today's Garbage Activities:

Lessons Learned From All This Garbage:

At Least The World Still Has:

...For Now.

Today's Ratings: ☆ ☆ ☆ ☆ ☆

Date: _____

Today's Garbage Humans:

Today's Garbage Activities:

Lessons Learned From All This Garbage:

At Least The World Still Has:

...For Now.

Today's Ratings: ☆ ☆ ☆ ☆ ☆
🗑 🗑 🗑 🗑 🗑

Date: _____

Today's Garbage Humans:

Today's Garbage Activities:

Lessons Learned From All This Garbage:

At Least The World Still Has:

...For Now.

Today's Ratings: ☆ ☆ ☆ ☆ ☆
🗑 🗑 🗑 🗑 🗑

Date: _____

Today's Garbage Humans:

Today's Garbage Activities:

Lessons Learned From All This Garbage:

At Least The World Still Has:

...For Now.

Today's Ratings: ☆ ☆ ☆ ☆ ☆
🗑 🗑 🗑 🗑 🗑

Date: _____

Today's Garbage Humans:

Today's Garbage Activities:

Lessons Learned From All This Garbage:

At Least The World Still Has:

...For Now.

Today's Ratings: ☆ ☆ ☆ ☆ ☆
🗑 🗑 🗑 🗑 🗑

Date: _____

Today's Garbage Humans:

Today's Garbage Activities:

Lessons Learned From All This Garbage:

At Least The World Still Has:

...For Now.

Today's Ratings: ☆ ☆ ☆ ☆ ☆
🗑 🗑 🗑 🗑 🗑

Date: _____

Today's Garbage Humans:

Today's Garbage Activities:

Lessons Learned From All This Garbage:

At Least The World Still Has:

...For Now.

Today's Ratings: ☆ ☆ ☆ ☆ ☆
🗑 🗑 🗑 🗑 🗑

Date: _____

Today's Garbage Humans:

Today's Garbage Activities:

Lessons Learned From All This Garbage:

At Least The World Still Has:

...For Now.

Today's Ratings: ☆ ☆ ☆ ☆ ☆

Date: _____

Today's Garbage Humans:

Today's Garbage Activities:

Lessons Learned From All This Garbage:

At Least The World Still Has:

...For Now.

Today's Ratings: ☆ ☆ ☆ ☆ ☆
🗑 🗑 🗑 🗑 🗑

Date: _____

Today's Garbage Humans:

Today's Garbage Activities:

Lessons Learned From All This Garbage:

At Least The World Still Has:

...For Now.

Today's Ratings: ☆ ☆ ☆ ☆ ☆
🗑 🗑 🗑 🗑 🗑

Date: _____

Today's Garbage Humans:

Today's Garbage Activities:

Lessons Learned From All This Garbage:

At Least The World Still Has:

...For Now.

Today's Ratings: ☆ ☆ ☆ ☆ ☆

Date: _____

Today's Garbage Humans:

Today's Garbage Activities:

Lessons Learned From All This Garbage:

At Least The World Still Has:

...For Now.

Today's Ratings: ☆ ☆ ☆ ☆ ☆

Date: _____

Today's Garbage Humans:

Today's Garbage Activities:

Lessons Learned From All This Garbage:

At Least The World Still Has:

...For Now.

Today's Ratings: ☆ ☆ ☆ ☆ ☆

🗑 🗑 🗑 🗑 🗑

Date: _____

Today's Garbage Humans:

Today's Garbage Activities:

Lessons Learned From All This Garbage:

At Least The World Still Has:

...For Now.

Today's Ratings: ☆ ☆ ☆ ☆ ☆
🗑 🗑 🗑 🗑 🗑

Date: _____

Today's Garbage Humans:

Today's Garbage Activities:

Lessons Learned From All This Garbage:

At Least The World Still Has:

...For Now.

Today's Ratings: ☆ ☆ ☆ ☆ ☆
🗑 🗑 🗑 🗑 🗑

Date: _____

Today's Garbage Humans:

Today's Garbage Activities:

Lessons Learned From All This Garbage:

At Least The World Still Has:

...For Now.

Today's Ratings: ☆ ☆ ☆ ☆ ☆
🗑 🗑 🗑 🗑 🗑

Date: _____

Today's Garbage Humans:

Today's Garbage Activities:

Lessons Learned From All This Garbage:

At Least The World Still Has:

...For Now.

Today's Ratings:

Date: _____

Today's Garbage Humans:

Today's Garbage Activities:

Lessons Learned From All This Garbage:

At Least The World Still Has:

...For Now.

Today's Ratings: ☆ ☆ ☆ ☆ ☆
🗑 🗑 🗑 🗑 🗑

Date: _____

Today's Garbage Humans:

Today's Garbage Activities:

Lessons Learned From All This Garbage:

At Least The World Still Has:

...For Now.

Today's Ratings: ☆ ☆ ☆ ☆ ☆
🗑 🗑 🗑 🗑 🗑

Date: _____

Today's Garbage Humans:

Today's Garbage Activities:

Lessons Learned From All This Garbage:

At Least The World Still Has:

...For Now.

Today's Ratings: ☆ ☆ ☆ ☆ ☆
🗑 🗑 🗑 🗑 🗑

Date: _____

Today's Garbage Humans:

Today's Garbage Activities:

Lessons Learned From All This Garbage:

At Least The World Still Has:

...For Now.

Today's Ratings: ☆ ☆ ☆ ☆ ☆
🗑 🗑 🗑 🗑 🗑

Date: _____

Today's Garbage Humans:

Today's Garbage Activities:

Lessons Learned From All This Garbage:

At Least The World Still Has:

...For Now.

Today's Ratings: ☆ ☆ ☆ ☆ ☆

Date: _____

Today's Garbage Humans:

Today's Garbage Activities:

Lessons Learned From All This Garbage:

At Least The World Still Has:

...For Now.

Today's Ratings: ☆ ☆ ☆ ☆ ☆
🗑 🗑 🗑 🗑 🗑

Date: _____

Today's Garbage Humans:

Today's Garbage Activities:

Lessons Learned From All This Garbage:

At Least The World Still Has:

...For Now.

Today's Ratings: ☆ ☆ ☆ ☆ ☆

🗑 🗑 🗑 🗑 🗑

Date: _____

Today's Garbage Humans:

Today's Garbage Activities:

Lessons Learned From All This Garbage:

At Least The World Still Has:

...For Now.

Today's Ratings: ☆ ☆ ☆ ☆ ☆

Date: _____

Today's Garbage Humans:

Today's Garbage Activities:

Lessons Learned From All This Garbage:

At Least The World Still Has:

...For Now.

Today's Ratings: ☆ ☆ ☆ ☆ ☆
🗑 🗑 🗑 🗑 🗑

Date: _____

Today's Garbage Humans:

Today's Garbage Activities:

Lessons Learned From All This Garbage:

At Least The World Still Has:

...For Now.

Today's Ratings: ☆ ☆ ☆ ☆ ☆
🗑 🗑 🗑 🗑 🗑

Date: _____

Today's Garbage Humans:

Today's Garbage Activities:

Lessons Learned From All This Garbage:

At Least The World Still Has:

...For Now.

Today's Ratings: ☆ ☆ ☆ ☆ ☆
🗑 🗑 🗑 🗑 🗑

Date: _____

Today's Garbage Humans:

Today's Garbage Activities:

Lessons Learned From All This Garbage:

At Least The World Still Has:

...For Now.

Today's Ratings: ☆ ☆ ☆ ☆ ☆
🗑 🗑 🗑 🗑 🗑

Date: _____

Today's Garbage Humans:

Today's Garbage Activities:

Lessons Learned From All This Garbage:

At Least The World Still Has:

...For Now.

Today's Ratings: ☆ ☆ ☆ ☆ ☆

Date: _____

Today's Garbage Humans:

Today's Garbage Activities:

Lessons Learned From All This Garbage:

At Least The World Still Has:

...For Now.

Today's Ratings: ☆ ☆ ☆ ☆ ☆
🗑 🗑 🗑 🗑 🗑

Date: _____

Today's Garbage Humans:

Today's Garbage Activities:

Lessons Learned From All This Garbage:

At Least The World Still Has:

...For Now.

Today's Ratings: ☆ ☆ ☆ ☆ ☆

Date: _____

Today's Garbage Humans:

Today's Garbage Activities:

Lessons Learned From All This Garbage:

At Least The World Still Has:

...For Now.

Today's Ratings: ☆ ☆ ☆ ☆ ☆

Date: _____

Today's Garbage Humans:

Today's Garbage Activities:

Lessons Learned From All This Garbage:

At Least The World Still Has:

...For Now.

Today's Ratings: ☆ ☆ ☆ ☆ ☆

🗑 🗑 🗑 🗑 🗑

Date: _____

Today's Garbage Humans:

Today's Garbage Activities:

Lessons Learned From All This Garbage:

At Least The World Still Has:

...For Now.

Today's Ratings: ☆ ☆ ☆ ☆ ☆

Date: _____

Today's Garbage Humans:

Today's Garbage Activities:

Lessons Learned From All This Garbage:

At Least The World Still Has:

...For Now.

Today's Ratings: ☆ ☆ ☆ ☆ ☆

Date: _____

Today's Garbage Humans:

Today's Garbage Activities:

Lessons Learned From All This Garbage:

At Least The World Still Has:

...For Now.

Today's Ratings: ☆ ☆ ☆ ☆ ☆
🗑 🗑 🗑 🗑 🗑

Date: _____

Today's Garbage Humans:

Today's Garbage Activities:

Lessons Learned From All This Garbage:

At Least The World Still Has:

...For Now.

Today's Ratings: ☆ ☆ ☆ ☆ ☆
🗑 🗑 🗑 🗑 🗑

Date: _____

Today's Garbage Humans:

Today's Garbage Activities:

Lessons Learned From All This Garbage:

At Least The World Still Has:

...For Now.

Today's Ratings: ☆ ☆ ☆ ☆ ☆
🗑 🗑 🗑 🗑 🗑

Date: _____

Today's Garbage Humans:

Today's Garbage Activities:

Lessons Learned From All This Garbage:

At Least The World Still Has:

...For Now.

Today's Ratings: ☆ ☆ ☆ ☆ ☆
🗑 🗑 🗑 🗑 🗑

Date: _____

Today's Garbage Humans:

Today's Garbage Activities:

Lessons Learned From All This Garbage:

At Least The World Still Has:

...For Now.

Today's Ratings: ☆ ☆ ☆ ☆ ☆
🗑 🗑 🗑 🗑 🗑

Date: _____

Today's Garbage Humans:

Today's Garbage Activities:

Lessons Learned From All This Garbage:

At Least The World Still Has:

...For Now.

Today's Ratings: ☆ ☆ ☆ ☆ ☆
🗑 🗑 🗑 🗑 🗑

Date: _____

Today's Garbage Humans:

Today's Garbage Activities:

Lessons Learned From All This Garbage:

At Least The World Still Has:

...For Now.

Today's Ratings: ☆ ☆ ☆ ☆ ☆
🗑 🗑 🗑 🗑 🗑

Date: _____

Today's Garbage Humans:

Today's Garbage Activities:

Lessons Learned From All This Garbage:

At Least The World Still Has:

...For Now.

Today's Ratings: ☆ ☆ ☆ ☆ ☆

Date: _____

Today's Garbage Humans:

Today's Garbage Activities:

Lessons Learned From All This Garbage:

At Least The World Still Has:

...For Now.

Today's Ratings: ☆ ☆ ☆ ☆ ☆
🗑 🗑 🗑 🗑 🗑

Date: _____

Today's Garbage Humans:

Today's Garbage Activities:

Lessons Learned From All This Garbage:

At Least The World Still Has:

...For Now.

Today's Ratings: ☆ ☆ ☆ ☆ ☆
🗑 🗑 🗑 🗑 🗑

Date: _____

Today's Garbage Humans:

Today's Garbage Activities:

Lessons Learned From All This Garbage:

At Least The World Still Has:

...For Now.

Today's Ratings: ☆ ☆ ☆ ☆ ☆
🗑 🗑 🗑 🗑 🗑

Date: _____

Today's Garbage Humans:

Today's Garbage Activities:

Lessons Learned From All This Garbage:

At Least The World Still Has:

...For Now.

Today's Ratings: ☆ ☆ ☆ ☆ ☆

Date: _____

Today's Garbage Humans:

Today's Garbage Activities:

Lessons Learned From All This Garbage:

At Least The World Still Has:

...For Now.

Today's Ratings: ☆ ☆ ☆ ☆ ☆
🗑 🗑 🗑 🗑 🗑

Date: _____

Today's Garbage Humans:

Today's Garbage Activities:

Lessons Learned From All This Garbage:

At Least The World Still Has:

...For Now.

Today's Ratings: ☆ ☆ ☆ ☆ ☆
🗑 🗑 🗑 🗑 🗑

Date: _____

Today's Garbage Humans:

Today's Garbage Activities:

Lessons Learned From All This Garbage:

At Least The World Still Has:

...For Now.

Today's Ratings: ☆ ☆ ☆ ☆ ☆
🗑 🗑 🗑 🗑 🗑

Date: _____

Today's Garbage Humans:

Today's Garbage Activities:

Lessons Learned From All This Garbage:

At Least The World Still Has:

...For Now.

Today's Ratings: ☆ ☆ ☆ ☆ ☆
🗑 🗑 🗑 🗑 🗑

Date: _____

Today's Garbage Humans:

Today's Garbage Activities:

Lessons Learned From All This Garbage:

At Least The World Still Has:

...For Now.

Today's Ratings: ☆ ☆ ☆ ☆ ☆

Date: _____

Today's Garbage Humans:

Today's Garbage Activities:

Lessons Learned From All This Garbage:

At Least The World Still Has:

...For Now.

Today's Ratings: ☆ ☆ ☆ ☆ ☆

Date: _____

Today's Garbage Humans:

Today's Garbage Activities:

Lessons Learned From All This Garbage:

At Least The World Still Has:

...For Now.

Today's Ratings: ☆ ☆ ☆ ☆ ☆
🗑 🗑 🗑 🗑 🗑

Date: _____

Today's Garbage Humans:

Today's Garbage Activities:

Lessons Learned From All This Garbage:

At Least The World Still Has:

...For Now.

Today's Ratings: ☆ ☆ ☆ ☆ ☆

🗑 🗑 🗑 🗑 🗑

Made in the USA
Columbia, SC
03 August 2020